What The Ancient Wisdom Expects of Its Disciples

A Study concerning the Mystery Schools

by

Manly Hall

Martino Fine Books
Eastford, CT
2017

Martino Fine Books
P.O. Box 913,
Eastford, CT 06242 USA

ISBN 978-1-68422-086-1

Copyright 2017
Martino Fine Books

Cover Design Tiziana Matarazzo

Printed in the United States of America On 100% Acid-Free Paper

What The Ancient Wisdom Expects of Its Disciples

A Study concerning the Mystery Schools

by

Manly Hall

HALL PUBLISHING CO.
LOS ANGELES, CAL.
1925

A WARNING TO ESOTERISTS

GREAT as is the number of present-day religious movements, both heterodox and orthodox, few of them inspire their followers to serve their fellow men along practical and intelligent lines. One by one the various cults are being involved in materialism and commercialism, among which by necessity they have been established. This is not to be wondered at, for it is difficult to separate our religion from our daily lives. We may call it by many different names, but it still reflects the thoughts and moral character of those who form its organization.

Modern attitudes on life are not healthy, and organizations built up by unhealthy people cannot be normal. Commercialism has attacked every plane of society. It has entered into all the walks of life. Our race is money mad. It is insane on the subject of personal gain. It will give nothing to serve others, but will give everything to gain the knowledge which will make it possible for the mediocre to become a commercial power overnight. The struggle inseparable from the ethics of competition is largely responsible for this condition. Graft has appeared in almost every walk of life. Nearly every existing institution is overrun by some mild form of moral dishonesty, and if every walk of life is commercialized and perverted, we cannot expect religion to escape.

History records no graft or prostitution equal to the grafts that today masquerade under the names of "psychology" and "new thought." The art of duping the public has evolved from the disreputable buffoonery of the Middle Ages to the polished pharisaism of the twentieth century. As seagulls follow a ship, so this curse has followed in the wake of that great wave of selfishness and moral perversion which is the product of our commercial age.

When correctly understood and properly used for the service of humanity, psychology, metaphysics, and new thought are highly commendable and their truths are sorely needed by ignorant humanity today. But what has happened? These names have been used to conceal all forms of mental, moral, spiritual, and physical infamy until everything we know of them today is a prostitution and commercialization of the truths for which they once stood. Their success is based upon the assumption that the people with whom they work are too ignorant to realize the injury that is being done.

We are not attacking the principles underlying these cults and philosophies nor the true thing for which the names stand. Neither are we attacking those sincere people who seek to assist others to build and unfold their characters. We are attacking perversion of truth and those persons who, shielding their crimes under the cloak of wisdom, deliberately and consciously mislead the public for the aggrandizement of self.

In the 14th chapter of St. John, 30th verse, Jesus states: "Hereafter I will not talk much with you; for the prince of this world cometh, and hath nothing in me." The Ancient Wisdom is not of this world; it belongs to an entirely different sphere. It is not interested in improving the material condition of the individual from the standpoint of placing him in executive positions or surrounding him with opulence. The Ancient Wisdom seeks to build the character of man, knowing that if he can be made right with himself, far more is accomplished than when he is made a ruler over many men.

Truth expresses the synthesis of the Divine Wisdom. Truth is the eternal reality of things. Psychology and metaphysics as taught today are not true, and the things taught under the guise of Truth are no better than those who disseminate them. An intellectual fact is not necessarily a truth; the misapplication of it is a falsehood.

If an individual wishes to take a course in business efficiency at the expense of others; if he wishes to attend a night school class in order to learn how to become a moral pickpocket, he is privileged to do so as long as he is willing to accept the Karmic consequences. You will remember that when Lucifer decided to rebel against God, the Deity allowed him to do so. It is demoralizing to a community for people to believe that God either gives or authorizes classes in slick salesmanship, shrewd bargaining, and mortgage foreclosing, or that He advocates sitting in the silence to get rid of an undesired marriage partner. Modern psychology has made God appear to be as dishonest as the persons who promulgate these doctrines. All this has a destructive effect on the life and health of the race. Let us consider a few points toward which the Ancient Wisdom was adamant and modern religion is lax. We can pick them from things going on around us all the time without going into abstractions.

1.   In all things involving the acquirement of knowledge, the Ancient Wisdom says, "First purify your own life." This means literally what it says. Until selfishness is removed from the soul of a student he can never hope to gain any knowledge that will serve him for any purpose more lofty than as a mental stimulant. The modern psychological cults overlook this entirely, failing to emphasize any virtue essential for the human nature outside of endless desires for things not normally attainable. Once men died for Truth, but now Truth dies at the hands of men.

2.   The Apostles who died for their faith, the Christians who sang in the arena while the lions were turned loose upon them, or who hung coated with tar as living torches in Nero's gardens—these furnished vivid demonstrations of the sincerity,

humility, honesty, and devotion of the early followers of Christ. The Master himself was led up into the mountain by the demons and tempted by a vision of the cities stretched out in the plains below. The ancient initiates were tempted by the things of this world. Buddha, standing beside the crib in which lay his infant son, chose between all the things which life held dear and the wandering life of an ascetic. But the great need of humanity filled his soul, and he sacrificed all to his great, unselfish love.

Again and again students are tempted by the voice of the world, and only if they are strong, will they gain that wisdom which they seek. The true occultist wants nothing but wisdom. When Solomon raised his hands to his God, Jehovah spoke from the heavens asking him what he would have, and he answered, "God give me the gift of wisdom." Jehovah asked him if there were not other things he desired, but Solomon answered, "No, only wisdom." And God told Solomon that because he had asked only for wisdom that all the other things should be added unto him and that from this day to the end of the world there would never be another king so rich, so great, or so blest. These are facts well worthy of consideration in the light of modem psychology.

As we listen to the words of the modern exponents of things divine, we see them making converts by offering to the ignorant the very things by which the ancient Masters were tempted by the demons of the air. Again and again the new cult leader promises his disciples the cities of the plains. His credulous followers fall over each other to study at his feet and learn how, through magnetic personalities or mental gymnastics, they can acquire the earthly possessions which he promises them. The crime does not lie in desiring the things of this world, for to a certain degree they are both necessary and good. Man would not be placed in his present environment unless he were expected to study and benefit by his experiences. The great crime lies in claiming these perverted doctrines to be spiritually inspired and representing God's chief desire to be making people financially independent.

3. Compare the initiates of days gone by, fighting a people who could not understand, struggling with idolatry and superstition and seeking to mold out of these things a truer and nobler concept of life, wandering day after day over the blistering sands like Moses in the wilderness—compare those master minds with the self-termed master minds of today and then ask yourself if you should follow them. The human race has never desired that which was best for it, but like a child it reaches out its hands and cries for the moon. Today the race does not know what is good for it, and individuals, instead of seeking to unfold their constitutions symmetrically, have gone mad over a system of philosophical hocus-pocus which promises something for nothing and exchanges divine wisdom for a moderate fee.

4. Without labor, there is no inspiration, and none can do our work for us but ourselves. The Ancient Wisdom demanded many years of purification and preparation before the adepts were willing to instruct in even the simplest things. Many modern occultists are glibly teaching Pythagorean mathematics and numerology, and if you come every afternoon for a week you will be greatly amazed how little you will discover. They wonder why it is that many of the keys of the Pythagorean mysteries have been lost to the world. The answer is simple. Pythagoras never instructed his disciples in any of his philosophical concepts until after they had passed through five years of the strictest discipline, among other things one provision being that during the entire time they were not to speak a word, in order that afterwards they might know how to hold their tongues. We would have much less trouble if our psychologists refrained from speaking for the first five years, for most of them are preaching with no more foundation for their eloquence than two weeks' study with

someone no better informed than themselves.

5. There is another class of people who go about discussing the Infinite with ease and fluency who as yet have never acquainted themselves with the finite. A most interesting rule of the Ancient Wisdom is that none of its initiates discuss the Absolute. They explain the hypothesis of First Cause, but state finally that no human being, themselves included, know sufficient concerning it to give an intelligent opinion or definition; and no wise man presumes to discuss that about which he knows nothing.

When Buddha was asked concerning the Absolute, he declined to discuss the subject. He was also silent concerning the gods, feeling that they were beyond the range of human intelligence. As a result, it has been said that he was an atheist, or at least a pantheist, when in reality it was his respect and reverence for Deity that led him, in his sublime wisdom, to refrain from giving utterance to words whose very inadequacy would but defile. When the disciples of Socrates questioned him concerning the Absolute, he also refused to discuss it, stating that it was beyond his wisdom and that it played no practical part in everyday life. But again and again fools dash in where angels fear to tread. While the greatest minds ever evolved by the human race dare not speak for fear they will desecrate that which is too sacred for words, some person, with neither record of accomplishment nor prospect of anything better, seeks to impress the uninformed by glibly discussing things he knows nothing about.

6. There is only one series of true occult exercises in the world—namely, esoteric exercises. Every nation has adopted these exercises with certain modifications to meet the needs of race, color, and organic qualities. The Christians took theirs from the Jews, the Jews from the Egyptians, the Egyptians from the Brahmans, and so on ad infinitum. When Buddha gave his faith to India he merely gave a doctrine for the consideration of the common people, for, being a Brahman himself, he followed

the Brahman culture of esoteric exercises. The so-called occult exercises are those formulas given by word of mouth by the initiates to their disciples under the pledge of absolute secrecy, in order that these disciples may use the exercises in spiritualizing, etherizing, and purifying their bodies.

One of the most reprehensible crimes perpetrated today is the teaching by present-day occultists of crazy, homicidal, and suicidal practices under the guise of esoteric instructions. If followed persistently, these practices will result in the death of those who attempt to follow them. The redeeming feature is that the average Western mind is incapable of concentrating long enough or consistently enough upon anything to be seriously harmed. All the esoteric instructions in the hands of unqualified people today are the result of treason and broken vows among the lower degrees of initiates. In order to receive them from such sources the recipient must become a party to the crime. Not only this, but when the student permits himself to listen to instructions gained falsely, he nullifies any good which he might otherwise gain.

Having obtained the instructions without the necessary preparation and apprenticeship ordered by the Great School, he cannot receive the spiritual insight that he desires. It breaks the hearts of the Masters to see people who know better dabbling with so-called esoteric exercises, gathering in circles to go into the silence, rolling their eyes into the tops of their heads and sitting in darkened rooms hoping to see something. It is not the mere fact that the student does these things which hurts the Teachers; it is the fact that the disciples have grown so little in discrimination that it is possible for them to become parties to such absurdities. We do not mean that they will not see things, hear voices, and gain certain mediumistic powers. We mean that they will be less useful after they have secured those powers than before, for they will have to unlearn again all those things and habits which they learned unwisely.

7. The Masters are ever waiting to entrust their disciples and students who show desire to receive with that wisdom which the world so sadly needs. If the student desires to go forth and teach, he will be given a work to do—that is, if he will honestly, sincerely, and intelligently prepare himself for his labors. The reason why so many false doctrines are being taught is that people who have an idea do not ask themselves, "Is this theory which I have, true? Am I living the sort of a life that would permit me to receive real truth into my soul? Am I unselfish, open, obedient, humble, and consecrated? Have I developed my mind so that it can think? Have I opened my heart so that it can feel? If I have not, then the thing which I have received is distorted by the glass through which it shines, and all I can give the world is a distorted image, a dishonest representation of truth. Have I actually consecrated my life and all that I am, unselfishly and without reservation, or am I only an intellectual dabbler? Am I a success or a failure in life? Am I surrounded by friends or by enemies of my own making? Am I respected by my community? Do I allow other people to live their own lives, or am I trying to force my beliefs upon all with whom I come in contact? Have I, or have I not, consciously and beyond all possibility of mental exaggeration, received personal instruction from the inner schools? I and I alone know that. The rest of the world, except the enlightened few, must believe what I say. If I have not received such instructions, am I big enough to admit it and say, with respect to my doctrines, that they are only my own opinions; or am I palming off these opinions as cosmic truths upon no firmer ground than the fact that I believe them?"

All these questions the student must ask himself, for he alone can answer them; but he is capable of injuring many if he is not honest in his statements concerning these fun- damental truths. If every teacher and student would thus interrogate himself, endless sorrow could be avoided, for he would realize that as an evil tree cannot bring forth good fruit, neither can a sin-filled body nor a perverted mind be the channel for the transmission of wisdom. Like begets like; the eccentric individual thinks eccentric thoughts, while the sane mind views all things sanely.

8. Psychologists today teach how one person may influence another to do things otherwise foreign to his nature. Let each student of the Mystery School be careful, therefore, when he studies with psychologists that the psychologist does not turn the tables on him. If he teaches you how to gain some advantage over another and twist that individual to your own ends, take care that he does not discover your gullibility and capitalize on you by way of demonstrating the application of his own philosophy. These things work both ways, and if you expect to psychologize others you must expect to be psychologized in turn; for it is a poor rule that does not work both ways. It is, however, a good rule which most people are willing to have turned around and applied to them. Psychology has psychologized the public and, like the children of Hamlin town who followed the Pied Piper, immature minds have followed false teachings until they have disappeared into the unknown.

9. Among the so-called students of truth we see the fruitage of the delusions from which the world suffers. Sickly, nervous, no longer capable of solving their own problems, they sit around treating each other, waiting like spiritual Micawbers for something to turn up. These people were once useful, intelligent members of their community, but they are now so involved in mental absurdities that they are useless both to themselves and to society in general. Most of all, they are like gaunt scarecrows who frighten others from the paths of wisdom.

10. The Ancient Wisdom is sane. It seeks to solve the problems with which we are surrounded today. It is spiritual and reasonable, in the highest sense of the word. It is seeking to

develop better men and women to meet the problems of future generations. It is based upon the law of cause and effect. It has no patented formulae, no shortcuts, but builds firmly and solidly the characters of those who unite themselves with its work. It is not led by mountebank teachers, but by great minds that have dedicated themselves since the beginning of the world to the promulgation of the sacred truths. It speaks with the experience of eternity, for it has led a thousand nations into being and buried as many when they turned from its course. The nations of antiquity which still exist are the ones which have preserved its laws, while those that have fallen are the ones that have ignored its commandments.

There is no greater honor than to be called to the service of this eternal Wisdom which was before the beginning and which will ultimately become the visible exoteric ruling body of the planet. Through the doors of its temple man passes from the temporal to the eternal, from ignorance to wisdom. It is strong and great, this Ancient Wisdom. It is the earth moistened with the waters of life in which are planted the seeds of doctrines, faiths, and religions. All these are dependent upon it for nourishment and growth. They blossom forth and are glorified, but the dark and mysterious soil in which they all grow is the Ancient Wisdom. From it they come; to it they will again return. They are temporal; it is eternal.

THE COMING OF THE
MYSTERY SCHOOLS

Since earliest times, the belief in a superior and supreme Being manifesting in totality what man manifests only in part has been the common property of human creatures. The mindless man struggling up through the muck and mire of the Paleozoic fens beat his hairy breast with long, misshapen arms and raised his cry to an unknown God. Even the hairy anthropoids of today have certain rudiments of religious worship. Soulless but aware, they turn their half-formed faces to the sky and clasp their hands as though in prayer. No one knows whence came the spirit of worship—the great desire to express thankfulness for the mere privilege of existing—but it is as old as history. The first writings are of the gods. Probably the first buildings were temples, for we are realizing   more day by day that every structure in Nature is a sanctuary built without the voice of workmen or the sound of hammers. It is not only a sanctuary but also an altar. It is not only the altar, but also the offering laid upon the altar. There is no voice, no people that does not bear witness to some God, some presence felt in the silence, some power seen in heaven.

All human beings are divided into four general classes, but each one lives in only one part of himself; or rather he minimizes all other portions and emphasizes this one above the rest. The lowest of these divisions is the physical nature, and those who dwell therein are of the earth, earthy; they live only for the gratification of their physical natures. Their idea of heaven is a place where there is food, feasting, and little or no work. They are the Brahmanic Sudras who, born in chains, are doomed to live and die in shackles of low organic quality. The very structure of the bones and flesh prohibits fineness in texture   either of body or soul. Their minds are only partly active. Their bodies resemble prisons more than dwelling places. They differ from the finer temperaments as the dray horse differs from the Arabian thoroughbred. Like the former, they live to labor, plodding along to a mediocre destiny. They are the laborers who must in truth earn their bread by the sweat of their brows. Give them opulence and they cannot retain it. Give them luxuries, and they do not appreciate them. They are the dark earthy ones who must ever bow before intelligence. They do not love God, for they cannot know Him. They are like the hairy anthropoids, raising their hands to unknown elements.

The second division is made up of the artisans and those who labor both with mind and hand. They are the brown men of the Indian myth. They buy, sell, and exchange. To their basic dullness has been added a certain cunning and some intelligence. Having a mind, they control the mindless. They are the petty shopkeepers and those of a similar class who are gradually exchanging the labor of the hand for the labor of the head. Not having the mental organism with which to reason, they fill the places of worship where thinking is done for them. They are the ones who allow their clergy to decide all spiritual problems for them, feeling themselves incapable of asssuming the onus of heavy thinking. As a result, their ideas of eternity are rather abstract and their credulity is utilized as a commercial asset by certain types of minds who consider it legitimate to capitalize on the ignorance of others.

The third class is made up of the scientists. With microscope, telescope, and other apparatus still more complex, they attack the boundary lines of the known and wage war upon the limitless chaos. Those who wage this war in the cause of science are mostly concrete thinkers who follow as far as their instruments will lead them and then must wait for instruments still more powerful. Most of these minds are atheistic or at least agnostic—that is, of course, unless they have two standards, one to last six days in the laboratory and the other to be assumed Sunday morning in church. The miracles of theology are incapable of chemical analysis and are consequently taken *cum grano salis* by the scientific world. Therefore the controversy between science and theology is bequeathed as a legacy to have and to hold upon that helpless posterity who come into the world to inherit the debate.

The fourth and highest group embraces philosophers, musicians, and artists, all living in an abstract mental world surrounded by dreams and visions wholly unrecognizable by the other types. They have reached beyond the world of academic education to the world of creative idealism, which is at present the highest function of the human mind. This world is the dwelling place of genius, of invention, and of the things which lower mentalities can only accept but never analyze. Religiously, these minds are deistic. Most of them are monotheists—believers in one God. Many of them are mystics or occultists, and, although possibly not yet sufficiently advanced to recognize their doctrines, yet belong to that finer type of mind capable of piercing the veil which divides the shadow from the substance.

In all human nature there is a certain expression of primitive instinct. With the desire for food which expresses the hunger of the material nature and the desire for freedom which expresses the hunger of the intellectual nature is also found that appreciation for the unknown—that aspiration which bears witness to the slumbering germ of a spiritual nature which somewhere in the constitution of all living things lies dormant and apparently lifeless.

As soon as man was capable of thought his mind turned upon himself. He sought to find a solution to the mystery of his own existence, which his unfolding intelligence was revealing to him in greater fullness every day. " What am I? Why am I here? What lies beyond the horizon line of futurity?" These were the great problems which confronted the primitive man, and these are also the great problems which confront the men and women of today.

Religions have gradually been evolved as man sought to explain himself. Once they were few and simple; now they are many and complicated. This in itself shows the ever-unfolding faculty range of the human mind. The primitive man could count up to only the number of his own fingers. Since then, however, the human mind has conceived mathematics, and by this science can now deal in infinite computations of numbers with at least some degree of intelligence. The greatest proof of the evolution of the human mind is found in the development of man's handiwork. The hollowed log of the primitive savage has become the great steamship of today. This great development which has gradually been brought about through the ages is not the result of the miraculous trans-   formation of natural substances but the gradual growth of the human mind, which is molding all it contacts into ever more complicated forms as the result of its ever-increasing senses and functions.

Religion is the outgrowth of many ages of spiritual hunger, when the soul of the primitive man, finding itself insufficient, turned in awe to the immensity of Nature, in whose endless pageantry it saw a power far greater than itself. The savage turned to the winds and found in them something superior to himself. He trembled in fear at the voice of the thunder; fell prostrate in terror as great storms swept through the primitive world and volcanic craters belched forth red-hot stones and ashes. He offered sacrifice to the gods of the air that they should spare him; he cried from the tops of the mountains and offered incense to the stars. He could not find God anywhere, so offered sacrifice to Him everywhere. He saw his crops burn for lack of water, his children sicken about him. His hopes were dashed to the ground by an unknown, unnamed thing which, though he could not understand, was the determining factor in every thought and action of his life. This was undoubtedly the origin of religion as man knows it. We remember the words of Pope: "Lo, the poor Indian! whose untutored mind sees God in clouds, or hears Him in the wind."

Man is small; Nature is great. Man is finite; Nature is infinite. Man struggling against Nature is like a tiny boat buffeted by the waves. In the endless grinding wheels of Nature ancient man recognized power. He realized that there was something greater than himself—a power that was supreme. He longed to exercise it, and through millions of years struggled, like Hiawatha and the Maize King, to extract from unknown power the secret of its greatness. Like Isis, he conjured Ra to tell his name and sought again and again to raise the veils of the World Virgin. He found that some things which he did destroyed him, while others brought him happiness and peace. He sought to learn which was which, and why, realizing that his very existence depended upon the wisdom of his choice.

Finding at last that he could not master Nature by force, he sought to master it through obedience. Our religious codes are largely the outcome of primitive experiments as the human mind, struggling for survival, gradually learned the will of Nature and molded itself into that will.

Today we are privileged to look back upon the history of the race and profit by the experience of the ages. Saints, sages, and saviors unnumbered have lived and died grappling with the problem of human destiny. The fruitage of their labors is preserved to us in the scriptures and philosophies of all nations. What are the so-called sacred books? Are they not merely the contributions to the knowledge of the world made by those who, devoting their lives to the problems of humanity and learning to solve them, have wandered alone yet unafraid in those causal worlds which man calls Nature?

Gradually man has built the body or institution he calls religion. It is a mental temple, its dome upheld by a number of columns, each of these columns one of the faiths of men. The East, the West, the North, and the South have contributed either to the strength or the beauty of that structure. The entire building, however, is a material thing. It is the offering of man to the Unknown. As the spirit enters the human body when the embryo reaches a certain degree of unfoldment, so will the spirit of Truth enter the religious body when that structure has adequately prepared itself for such a coming.

The world knows many religions, but Nature has but one Truth. All so-called faiths and doctrines are contributing   to the knowledge of that one Truth. All are expressing one ideal through a multitude of tongues. There is a babel on the earth, but there is only one voice in the heavens. All faiths are seeking to answer one question: "What is the purpose of existence?" Each answers it differently. When all are gathered together in their diversities, Truth is established, for Truth is the sum of all these things. Reality is all things unto all men.

The Ancient Wisdom is the invisible, spiritual side of religion which quickens the body of religion. It is the one spirit which speaks through a multitude of tongues. It is that presence which enters in when its temple has been built by the body of its work-men. It vivifies the body of faith, making it alive and not merely a series of empty shells. Like the gods of India, it has many arms and many heads, but only one heart.

In the very early period of human differentiation, man was incapable of self-government, but was ruled by those appointed by Nature to preserve him and unfold him to the point when he would be capable of taking care of himself. We are told that when our solar system began its labors, spirits of wise beings from other solar systems came to us and taught us the ways of wisdom that we might have that birthright of knowledge which God gives to all His creations. It was these minds which are said to have founded the Mystery Schools of the Ancient Wisdom, for this Wisdom was the knowledge of the will of Nature for Her children.

The greatest art in all the world is the art of being natural, for that which is natural shall survive. For ages religion has been founded upon a false hypothesis. It has sought to fill the world with miracles and unnatural things. It has sought to dictate and dogmatize. For this reason it is failing. Religion is a body, but today it is a soulless body. It has not built its tabernacle according to the law. It is not serving intelligently and honestly the needs of the human race, but rather is involving itself and its members in endless dissensions of creed, doctrines, and codes, forgetting entirely the spirit of Truth. As a result, one of the most important elements of human life is gradually removing itself from the world; and for lack of an honest, intelligent, fair-minded, and progressive religion we have an age of extreme materialism when the God of man merely changes from a gilded figure of an unknown God to a gilded coin with distinctly practical uses.

The Ancient Wisdom tells us that there is but one religion and that its seed was planted in the souls of things with the beginning of the world. It became a mighty tree with its roots in heaven and its branches on earth, like the sacred banyan of India. As all the branches depend upon one trunk, so all faiths and religions depend upon one source, one light for all that they have been, are, or ever shall be. Some branches are large and strong, while others are small and weak, but through all of them courses one life. That life is light, and that light is the life of men.

The Ancient Wisdom knows neither heathen, nor Christian, nor pagan. It recognizes only many branches on one tree, each branch in itself incomplete but each part of the Tree of Faith. The Tree asks nothing of the branches, other than that they shall be true to the Tree and bear true witness of the life coursing through the Tree. The Ancient Wisdom is the life in the Tree of Faith. We do not see the life. We see only the leaves and branches which bear witness to the life, but in due season the miracle of the tree is accomplished. The life of the tree is glorified in the bud and in the flower. The life of the tree is consummated in the fruit of the tree. The glory of the life of that tree is in the new seed which bears full witness to the creative power of all that has gone before.

This tree is indeed a Tree of Life, for without the higher and finer sentiments man does not live; he merely exists. If any branch of that tree does not bear fruit, the Master tells us that it shall be cut off and cast into the fire. It is the duty of all living things to produce some truly constructive labor as recognition of the divine life which is within them. God is most glorified when His children glorify His spirit within themselves.

In the remote past the gods walked with men and while the instructors from the invisible planes of Nature were still laboring with the infant humanity of this planet, they chose from among the sons of men the wisest and the truest. These they labored with, preparing them to carry on the work of the gods after the spiritual hierarchies themselves had withdrawn into the invisible worlds. With these specially ordained and illumined sons they left the keys of their great wisdom, which was the knowledge of good and evil. They ordained these anointed and appointed ones to be priests or mediators between themselves (the gods) and that humanity which had not yet developed the eyes which permitted them to gaze into the face of Truth and live.

Overshadowed by the divine prerogative, these illumined ones, founded what we now know as the Ancient Mysteries. These were schools of religious truths, religion being here used in its sense of implying divine wisdom. To these spiritual universities were admitted the most worthy and most capable of the sons of men. At first these schools were publicly recognized. Great temples were built to house the priests and serve as chambers of initiation. The record of the mystical arcane was in the form of carvings, baked clay tablets, and papyrus rolls. Generation after generation was illumined by the wisdom secreted in these sacred repositories.

Gradually a separation took place among the schools of the Mysteries. The zeal of the priests to spread their doctrines in many cases apparently exceeded their intelligence. As a result, many were allowed to enter the temples before they had really prepared themselves for the wisdom they were to receive. The result was that these untutored minds, slowly gaining positions of authority, became at last incapable of maintaining the institution because they were unable to contact the spiritual powers behind the material enterprise. So the Mystery Schools vanished. The spiritual hierarchy, served through all generations by a limited number of true and devoted followers, withdrew from the world; while the colossal material organizations, having no longer any contact with their divine source, wandered in circles, daily becoming more involved in the rituals and symbols which they had lost the power of interpreting.

An interesting and concrete example of the deterioration of the Mystery Schools and their rituals is found in the children's Punch and Judy play. For hundreds of years the frivolous of all Western nations have laughed at the strange antics of these little figures. The world has long forgotten that this play originated among the early Christian mystics, where Punch was Pontius Pilate and Judy was Judas Iscariot. The little club which Punch carries is a degeneration of the ancient scepters which were carried by Roman dignitaries in the Holy Land. It is also quite probable that the famous scene between Punch and the baby is taken from the early Christian story of the Slaughter of the Innocents.

It is really remarkable how down through the ages, by word of mouth, by allegory and symbol, and by natural example, the truths revealed to the ancients have been perpetuated to our own day and yet have ever been concealed from the eyes of the profane. It has been said that wisdom lies not in seeing things but in seeing through things. For the occultist at least, this is doubly true.

During the Atlantean periods of which Plato dreamed, the work of gathering and arranging the Ancient Wisdom went on apace, for the people of Atlantis were the greatest exponents of concrete thought the world has ever known. The Atlanteans never fully understood the wisdom that was theirs, for even in those early times the gods had withdrawn from the mass of humanity, and spoke to man only through appointed priests and oracles. The method of communication used by the spiritual powers is faithfully set out by Josephus in his description of the Ark of the Covenant and the priests who served it. This ark was an oracle, and the gods spoke to the high priest by means of the language of symbolism. From the Atlanteans, with their ancient Tabernacle Mysteries, we have secured nearly all that we know concerning the Ancient Wisdom and its Mysteries. According to the Sacred Book, they were the keepers of the spiritual records which had been given to them by their progenitors, the Serpent Kings, who reigned over the earth.

It was these Serpent Kings who founded the Mystery Schools which later appeared as the Egyptian and Brahman Mysteries and other forms of ancient occultism. The serpent was their symbol, for they taught man the use of the creative energy which courses through Nature and his own bodies as a serpentine line of force. They were the true Sons of Light, and from them have descended a long line of adepts and initiates duly tried and proven according to the law. These have kept alight the divine truths through many generations of ignorance and thoughtlessness. The later Atlantean world crumbled because it wavered from the law. It forgot that Nature was the ruler of all things, and in attempting to survive unnaturally it was destroyed. Before its disintegration, however, the Ancient Wisdom passed into the new Aryan world, where from the heart of the lofty Himalayas its adepts and initiates began the process of building a new people to be the living tabernacles of the gods among men.

Man has not always been a material being. Eternities ago he was a spiritual creature, of radiant and glorious powers. Gradually he assumed the coats of skins which we call bodies, and his radiance was darkened by the sheaths of clay. Little by little he lost touch with his Fathers, the Sons of Light, and began to wander in darkness. At the time when the third eye closed in man, during the period of the ancient Lemurian world, the human race lost contact with its invisible teachers. Gradually even the memory of them faded out until only myths and legends remained. Mythology is the authentic record of those periods of transition when the diviner sparks were gradually assuming the bodies of mortality.

But man was never left to wander alone in ignorance. When the ties connecting him to the unseen worlds were broken, certain methods were established whereby the will of the gods could be made known. To this end, a certain number of men and women were instructed how to bridge the chasm which then separated the gods from men. The method of establishing this communication was the greatest of all the secrets of ancient occultism. This secret has been preserved for the race, for at a later time all human beings will be able to communicate directly with the gods once more. During the great interval of ages, this wisdom has been perpetuated in the Mystery Schools, and a few chosen disciples in each generation have been given the sacred privilege of knowing the gods. This wisdom and the power and knowledge they have gained they in turn impart to a few chosen and beloved disciples. Thus the work is carried on.

The ability of the Mystery Schools to communicate with the invisible worlds is the basis of their power; for all the creative hierarchies dwell in the unseen worlds, and there the disciple must go in order to consult them. The reason for this is that the human race is the only one in our scheme of things that is equipped with both a physical and a mental body. The gods, so-called, have never descended into physical substance. Consequently, having no body composed of dense chemical elements, they are incapable of manifesting here. In order to communicate with them, man must, therefore, learn to function consciously in his own invisible bodies. When he is capable of doing this, he can communicate with the spiritual beings who dwell in similar superphysical substances. Thus, while religion deals only with fancies, theorems, and beliefs, the initiates of the Ancient Wisdom go straight to the fountainhead of wisdom and, learning the will of the gods, make that will the law of their lives. The initiate does not guess, wonder or soliloquize; he labors with facts for he is one with the truths of Nature.

The secret path of spiritual illumination is the way which the planetary Logos has established that His children might learn to know of Him and accomplish His ends. The Logos is surrounded by a hierarchy of superhuman beings and also by a group of great initiates who may be called the fruitage of the human world period. These great initiates, with their divinely-inspired minds, are established as mighty pillars in the House of their God. They are the supports of the Temple of Human Progress. These great minds were called by the ancient Jewish mystics "The Cedars of Lebanon." These are the trees which Solomon is supposed to have cut from the forests of earth to use as the mainstays of his divine temple.

From north, east, south, and west the secret truths of these initiated minds have been gathered. The adepts and mystics of all nations have given to their disciples the fruitage of their investigations while functioning in the invisible worlds. The Mysteries Schools, fulfilling the ancient law, are fashioned in the pattern of Nature, and we know them today as the seven Great Schools of the Mysteries. All these are branches of one tree which grows in the center of the Garden of the Lord, watered by the four rivers (the wisdom of the four worlds). As every ray of light breaks into seven colors when it strikes a prism, so this ancient truth, striking the prismatic body of the material world, appears in a septenary body. This body is called the seven-headed serpent, for although it speaks with seven mouths it has but one brain, one life, one origin.

The priests of the Mysteries were symbolized as a serpent, sometimes called Hydra. From this word we have secured our common word, hydrant. As the hydrant carries water, so through the hydra-body of the initiate pass the waters of life. He is, therefore, a tube or channel through which they are disseminated like water from the nozzle of a hydrant.

These seven schools, each composed of twelve initiates and their disciples surrounding a thirteenth exalted brother, are the God-ordained perpetuators of the Ancient Wisdom as it has come from the dawn of the world when the gods descended from the nebula of the sun and took up their dwelling place on the sacred island at the north polar cap.

As this document is not intended for propaganda purposes, we shall not name any of these schools, but they represent the seven planets and the seven great paths. They represent also the seven vital organs of the human body and the seven vials which pour out their contents upon the world. All disciples seeking to gain knowledge concerning the laws of Nature must secure that wisdom through one of these seven channels appointed by the

Infinite for the furtherance of His peculiar work. Every one of these Mystery Schools is invisible and unknown. They can only be found after long searching and repeated disappointment. In recognition of the dignity of these schools and the sanctity of the wisdom which they represent, this treatise has been prepared to give in a simple way some of the marvelous truths for which they stand.

Every hundred years the voice of the Great School is heard, and into the world comes one to bear witness to the unseen. He speaks with the voice of wisdom, and he is overshadowed by the seven lights. Gradually the Mystery School (the seven branches considered as a unit) is leavening the entire loaf of human thought. Today as never before men are turning to search for their gods; or we should say they are rather turning away in disgust from our age of materiality which is slowly crushing the beauty and spirituality out of life. Our materiality is destroying the souls of men; it is breaking the heart of the world; it is stifling the finer side of every nature, and something within man is revolting against this unnatural oppression. Many who have never given it thought before   are now wondering what the end of it all will be, how far the human race can involve itself without bringing the entire structure of modern ethics crashing down in ruins.

Within the last fifty years, thousands have become spiritual pilgrims and taken up their search for truth, seeking amid the hills and valleys of the human soul for the answer to the riddle of destiny. They are seeking for those mystic Masters of Wisdom known to legend but of whom history bears no record. Throughout all this searching there is a great uncertainty, but one or two facts stand out very clearly. First, the majority of people do not know what they are looking for. If they should meet truth, they would not recognize it. The Masters they seek are about them every day; but like Sir Launfal they journey into distant lands, seeking for those things which are upon their own doorsteps. Secondly, they would not accept wisdom if they should find it. They would all be glad to have the power that the Masters have, but few would labor unselfishly and untiringly for ages to secure that power and then consecrate it unreservedly to the good of humanity.

Before passing on to our next subject, let us sum up a few points to be remembered concerning the Great Work and its workers in the world.

1. The instinct of reverence for the Unknown is implanted in all human life. It seems that even many of the higher animals must have it, for as they sit at the feet of their beloved masters their animal souls speak through upturned eyes filled with love and tenderness. The love of the dog for its master and the love of the disciple for his teacher are closely allied. The dog asks for nothing but kind words and will lay down its life for its master.

Such is true devotion. From the savage upward, reverence and devotion to the gods form part of the moral code of all humanity. Many may deny it, but in the form of either faith, fear, or superstition it persists.

2. The Maker of the great plan which we call life, the Being from which we have been differentiated, has given man certain potentialities; these when awakened to dynamic powers will give to each the faculties whereby he may know that plan. By learning it himself and applying his wisdom, he may then reach the position where he can assist others to harmonize their lives with the same law.

3. For the purpose of disseminating this wisdom wisely among all the nations of the earth, the Schools of the Ancient Mysteries have been established, not by the will of man but by the gods themselves laboring through channels chosen from the

most highly evolved children of earth.

4. Having established these schools, the superior intelligences became the central invisible powers of these schools and are still in actual communication with the Adepts and Masters who at the present time manipulate the destinies of these secret orders.

5. All growth spiritually must take place through one of the seven channels appointed by Nature for that purpose, and at some stage in his spiritual growth each disciple will enter the planetary path best fitted to evolve the qualities that lie dormant within himself.

6. These seven schools, together with their branches in all parts of the earth, constitute the Great White Lodge. This is the divine institution appointed to give the Ancient Wisdom to our planet. It is composed of all of the initiates and adepts of the White Path and forms the invisible government of the earth.

7. The Ancient Wisdom contains the true and accurate knowledge of the plan whereby the gods, man and the universe were established, are being maintained, and will later be dissolved into eternity. It is the knowledge of all things in their relation to God, Nature and themselves, and it is the only guide by which man can be shown the path he must follow if he would liberate himself from the ignorance and darkness of materiality.

8. Anyone may walk that path who will accept and live up to the obligations which the Ancient Wisdom places upon all who would learn the mysteries of life and death. If they will live the life which it points out, they shall know not only the doctrine which it preaches but also the Great Ones who have been chosen by their own virtues to teach their younger brethren the Ancient Wisdom.

THE MYSTERY SCHOOLS

In all the schools of the Ancient Wisdom the members are divided into three general classes or groups. Every seeker after truth is in one of these divisions, whether conscious of it or not. The esoteric teachings of all religions are the same. The ends to be attained are identical in every case. The only difference between them is that each school is especially fitted to reach and work with the type of mind and body of the people among whom it is established. In other words, we may say that the Mystery Schools interpret truth along the lines of the familiar, clothing wisdom in symbol and allegory familiar to those who are supposed to receive it. All the schools demand the same inflexible standards of consecration and virtue, teaching that each student and candidate must build his own character, unfold his own spiritual powers, and control his own lower nature before he can receive assistance from any superior source.

When little children come into this world they are sent to our public and private schools in order to prepare themselves intelligently for their period of activity here. While they are young and uninformed, their parents protect them, but when they reach maturity they are expected to assume the responsibilities of life and help others as they themselves have been assisted. No one is born without responsibility. *Each living thing is responsible for itself,* and when it fails to assume its individual responsibilities others must suffer as well as the thoughtless one.

As growing children are instructed in the laws governing their environments in order that they may intelligently assist in molding the destiny of the race, so the Mystery Schools are instructing those children of men who desire to know the laws that govern the unseen world. These laws, although entirely unknown to the average individual, play an important part in everyday life. The Mystery Schools are universities where the spiritual nature is unfolded and trained, and man is prepared to become an active worker in the great plan of cosmic progress.

The world we live in is a world of effects. Around us, but invisible, are the worlds of causation. They are the realities, while the visible, which lives through the power of the invisible, is the illusion. No matter how deeply we study the material arts and sciences, we can never find out the real cause of anything. Science is still seeking and will continue to search indefinitely for a real foundation upon which to work.

The four great questions upon which all knowledge should be based remain unanswered, and science is forced to admit that they are beyond the scope of modern mentality. What is life? What is consciousness? What is force? What is mind? None can answer, for these are invisible things, incapable of being measured or analyzed, consequently no material mind incapable of reason beyond the point of concrete vision will ever solve their riddle.

If we would step across the line which divides the true from the false, the spiritual from the material, the eternal from the temporal, we must realize that the Mystery Schools were established in the world so that this transition might be possible. Through the special instruction and understanding gained by membership and graduation from these institutions, man is enabled to become a citizen of two worlds, for the schools themselves are of two worlds. Their gateways are in the material world, otherwise none would know that they exist; but the temples themselves are in the spiritual substances of Nature. In order to reach these temples, candidates must learn to function in the so-called invisible substances. The worlds of causation are invisible only because they are beyond the range of our sense perceptions. *By certain forms of culture,* however, it is possible to develop sense perceptions at present latent in the average individual. These senses, being more   highly evolved than those we ordinarily use, are capable of studying and exploring the so-called causal worlds.

As power is given to man commensurate to his wisdom and understanding, it is not safe at the present time to reveal to the world at large the methods whereby entrance to the invisible world is possible. If this knowledge were given to selfish people unprepared for their responsibility, they would be able to destroy the universe, either through perversion or ignorance. In order to protect this sacred wisdom obstacles have been placed in the way of its attainment which only the sincere and courageous would be strong enough to overcome. Years of service, self-purification and self-mastery must be passed through before any candidate will be admitted to the path of wisdom.

Three steps (degrees) lead up to the temple door, and all who wish to enter, whatever their race or their religion, must climb them. There is no other legitimate way of gaining wisdom. Those who seek to enter the Temple of the Mysteries by any way other than the gate appointed by the Masters, the same are thieves and robbers. Man is willing to spend from ten to fifteen years on his material education in order that he may surpass his fellow man in some pursuit. Should he, then, expect to attain his spiritual wisdom in any shorter time?

The position a person occupies in the Mystery Schools is not the result of choice, ballot or election; *it is his life and the way that he lives it that is the determining factor in all his spiritual studies.* He is automatically placed upon the path of wisdom according to his vices and virtues. The rapidity of his advancement depends wholly upon his own   merits—the sincerity, integrity, and devotion which marks his daily life. He may remain many years in one grade or pass like a comet through many grades in a few years. This depends entirely on how sincerely and honestly he has labored and how completely he has mastered the temperaments and failings which hold him back.

The three divisions into which disciples of the Great Work are divided are given to us out of great antiquity. They are the same divisions that we find among the priests of the tabernacle of the Jews; they are the same as the caste divisions of India, and many others. We may consider them under three headings, as follows:

The first degree is that of Student. This is the lowest of the three grades of the Mystery Schools, and is composed of persons of either sex who have accepted the Masters of Wisdom and their work of unfolding human consciousness as the greatest reality in life and who have, of their own free will, joined themselves to the cause of human progress. This does not mean that they have sworn adherence to any individual or material organization. It means that they have sanctified their lives and dedicated their efforts to humanitarian service, which is the true path of mastery and the only road which escapes the pitfalls of egotism and commercialism.

Service is a great word. It means a devotion to the needs of the masses which is so strong, perfect, and unselfish that wealth, honors, and all things this world holds dear, will be given up instantly, gladly, and without the sense of sacrifice in the service of the ideal it has espoused. The class of student includes all who think, read, study, and aspire along the lines of the Ancient Wisdom. In its ranks are all so-called independent occultists, various kinds of untrained psychics, mediums, psychologists and others who have no direct connection with the teachers from any division of the Great School but who are seeking according to their own light to understand the initiates words as they have heard them or found them recorded in literature.

In this group we also find many student teachers who, while not initiated into the Mysteries, are seeking to assist others on the path of wisdom. Such a one was Socrates, who, while himself ignorant concerning many things, gave to the world two of its greatest initiates, Plato and Aristotle.

The student is generally without any actual proof of the thing he believes. Some intuitive voice within, however, tells him that the studies he is laboring with are true. He must so accept them. The privilege of knowing the reason for the things that he does, is not given to him as yet. He must obey blindly the great laws as they are revealed to him and await the pleasure of the Elder Brothers. During these years of spiritual darkness he must spend his life in self-improvement along those lines which he normally recognizes as virtuous and true. He must consecrate himself to the labor of preparing his nature for the greater responsibilities that are to come.

Over a hundred years ago a great disciple of alchemy and magical philosophies compiled a series of suggestive rules for those who desire to become true students of wisdom. We have extracted from the writings of Francis Barrett the following thoughts (not quoted in full):

Lesson I. Learn to cast away from thee all vile affections ... and in constancy of mind let all thy dealings be free from deceit and hypocrisy.

Lesson II. Keep thine own and thy neighbor's secrets; court not the favors of the rich; despise not the poor, for he who does will be poorer than the poorest.

Lesson III. Give to the needy and unfortunate what little thou canst spare; for he that has but little, whatever he spares to the miserable, God shall amply reward him.

Lesson IV. Be merciful to those who offend thee or who have injured thee; for what shall the man's heart be who would take heavy vengeance on a slight offense? Thou shalt forgive thy brother until seventy times seven.

Lesson V. Be not hasty to condemn the actions of others, lest thou shouldst, the next hour, fall into the very same error; despise scandal and tattling; and let thy words be few.

Lesson VI. Study day and night and supplicate thy Creator that He would be pleased to grant thee knowledge and understanding.

Lesson VII. (Omitted as irrelevant.)

Lesson VIII. Avoid gluttony and all excess—it is very pernicious, and from the Devil: these are the things that constantly tempt man, and by which he falls a prey to his spiritual adversary; for he is rendered incapable of receiving any good or divine gift.

Lesson IX. Covet not much gold, but learn to be satisfied with enough; for to desire more than enough is to offend the Deity."

These rules for spiritual propriety are as good today as when they were first written, and should be deeply considered by all students, for all things come to man by attraction and if seeds of wisdom and virtue are not within himself, the gods can bestow nothing upon him. The duty of every student of the Ancient Wisdom is to make himself valuable to his fellow men, for when he does this he makes himself valuable to the plan of Nature.

The student must always realize that he is preparing himself to become the hands and feet of Wisdom, for when Wisdom enters into the soul of man the wise becomes its servant. The student must always bear witness to the divine urge of progress. He must train his mind, control his appetites, and make himself a well-balanced example of human growth. His intellectual pursuits should be largely along lines which will assist him in his judgment of human nature. He should study both people and things. He should not become a recluse, for if he loses touch with the world and the things of the world he cannot efficiently serve that which he has given up.

His study is to view life as a place and a time for learning, realizing that wisdom is the jewel to be extracted from material existence. He must always keep in mind that he is not studying for himself alone but is building for the day when, his long years of preparation finished, his wisdom will be used by still greater powers to assist in those great problems which ever confront the world.

Every student should seek to develop talents. He should try to make two blades of grass grow where one has grown before. He must become a creative genius, an outstanding example of intelligence in the highest sense of the word. But it should always be unselfishly. He should never become attached either to the work he is doing or to the positions that he occupies, for the Master may call him to other labors at any moment. If he can legitimately and honestly become a power in the community wherein he dwells, he should assume such responsibilities, for they offer greater opportunities for the accomplishment of the greatest good to the greatest number.

It is not expected that a student should have clairvoyant powers or any personal spiritual abilities. *In fact, it is better that he should not, lest in his unenlightened ignorance he pervert them.* Students seeking to gain various forms of mediumship and psychism by occult exercises and mantrams, should take warning. (One of the Masters of wisdom has distinctly stated that all forms of phenomenalism are to be rejected by the student). He must build a spiritual, mental nature, and not merely allow his emotional palate to be tickled by weird phenomena. No true student of any legitimate Master should ever attempt to converse either with the living or the dead through mediumistic powers.

Some schools have made it clear that students will forfeit their right to instruction by seeking to communicate with the departed or by indulging in similar forms of psychism).

The student is not expected to be a great occultist or a great mystic. Such aspirations belong only to the higher grades. It is, however, demanded by the Masters of the student that he shall be simple, humble, honest, and patient, struggling daily to gain mastery with the true virtue over the undesirable traits of his own nature.

He is not in a position to dictate what the Masters will have him do. He must accept unquestioningly the responsibilities that are given to him of the great Unknown, and fulfill each of them as honestly and thoroughly as lies in his power. At this period of probationship the student is gaining mastery over the little things. Let him make sure that he is successful. Let him struggle to control the sharp tongue, the critical mind, and the abnormal viewpoints, that they shall not later bring dishonor upon the Spirit of Truth when it shall come to dwell within his nature.

The true student is cutting out a finer character from the rough ashlar that has been given him. He is struggling to improve each day just a little, asking not for power or light but for strength to shape his destiny more truly to the standards of Wisdom. These are the labors of the student. His worthiness to receive greater knowledge is tested by long years of ignorance, often by much suffering. Through all he must be obedient, patient, and true, realizing that each sorrow is an opportunity, each misfortune a lesson in disguise. These lessons he must learn; when this task has been done, they vanish to return no more.

When he offers himself to the Master's service, the student is filled with unworthy thoughts and elements. Behind him stretch many ages of thoughtlessness and crime. His higher bodies are a mass of bad Karma, and he is totally unfitted for his labors.

Before wisdom can be given to him, it is necessary that his evil nature be cleansed. So the Masters give him the labor of purifying himself as the first test of his sincerity. All that follows depends on how that first work is accomplished.

Thus his consecration often results in years of sorrow for the student; but everything has its price in Nature, and a cleansed soul is the price of wisdom, for it is only a balanced and honest nature that can honestly think or honestly analyze. All the perversions of the past present their bills and demand payment. A great spiritual housecleaning follows, for all these bills must be paid. No true religion teaches a student that these debts can be escaped. A man does not avoid his responsibilities by becoming spiritual. He is merely given the privilege of paying his debts sooner. In this great truth Christianity has been false to its founder, for Christianity as we have it today is a religion of vicarious atonements, until in referring to the spiritual status of the average Christian, one of the Masters stated: "The pauper angels of the Christian heavens." If the student takes up the Ancient Wisdom to escape his sins, he fails before he begins; for the Masters want only honest men and women in their service and all honest people shoulder their own responsibilities.

As the result of this unexpiated Karma, the path of studentship is often beset with infirmity and suffering, but these things are the tests which prove the character of the candidate. He will be accepted by the Masters only if his character survives these misfortunes and comes through them deepened and mellowed by the experiences. The student must labor year after year, waiting in patience and perfect trust until he has so far succeeded that he is found worthy to receive instruction from one of the Masters of their disciples.

No student knows when that moment will be, nor should he desire it to be hastened. His present labor is to serve to the best of his ability. In the hands of those wiser than himself he has entrusted his destiny and his immortal spirit, and in patience he awaits their pleasure. His province is to do; theirs to judge the doing.

The second degree is that of Disciple. In this grade are the accepted *chelas* "students" of an Initiate, Master or *Guru.* For them the veil is beginning to lift. They have placed their feet firmly upon the winding path that leads to the Temple of one of the seven Great Schools. Instead of wandering far in the search for wisdom, they gather at the feet of their appointed Master and learn from him.

Today in occult work there is too much wandering from one place to another, too much uncertainty in the soul of the student. Let him choose one path and, having established the integrity of the teacher and the teaching, remain with that.

One day while the student was laboring in the vineyard of life, tired but faithful and patient withal, the Master came that way and stopped to watch the student at his work. The student was singing at his toil. Each thing he did was accomplished with love and sincerity. Trust, hope, and consecration were his tools. He was laboring not for himself but for his brother and his God. Accompanying every act was a prayer—a silent consecration of the work of his hands and the meditations of his heart to that great invisible Thing in whom he lived and moved and had his being.

The heavier the load, the greater his joy, for he was doing good. All this and other things the Master saw. But the student did not see the Teacher, for the sweat from the laborer's brow ran down into his eyes and blinded him. The Master stepped over to the student, saying, "Leave now your labors and follow me." The vineyard vanished, the dirt fell from the hands of the worker, and for a moment he dwelt in space, while before him was the shining figure of his Master. He sank on his knees at the feet of the Master and kissed the hem of his robe. Again the

Master spoke: "You are my disciple. You have not chosen me; I have chosen you. You have been faithful unto a few things; now you shall have power over more and greater things."

Thus is the disciple chosen by his Master and brought into personal contact with the Teacher, his cosmic benefactor. Each Master has a number of disciples, usually twelve. They are his chosen sons. He becomes their father, and they leave all else and cling unto him. As our physical fathers and mothers bring us into the physical world and help us build our bodies here, so the Masters give us birth into the unseen spiritual worlds and assist us to build our superphysical vehicles so that we may function there. For this the Master is both father and mother, and more; for he gives us eternal birth while our material parents bring us only into the illusion.

The disciple does not choose his Master; it is the Master who calls his disciples from their various labors to follow him. None not actually and actively engaged in the vineyard of life will ever be called to the greater work. For the disciple the day of book-learning is over. The day of personal investigation is at hand. He has been accepted, and now the spiritual worlds centralize upon him and help him in every possible way. We may say that the disciples are the esoteric students. They are those who, having been weighed in the balances, have been found not wanting. They have reached that point when the discerning eye of the Initiate notes their sincerity and they are accepted as beyond the liability of failure.

The Master, after making a personal examination of the auric bodies of his disciples, gives them individual instruction concerning the preparation through which they must go before they can be admitted into the Great School itself.

It is this Teacher, the beloved *Guru*, and this one alone, who has the power and right to prescribe any form of occult exercises such as meditation, concentration, breathing, chanting, visualizing, and so forth. Students show very poor discrimination when they allow strangers interested only from a commercial standpoint to prescribe any form of spiritual exercise for them. They prove by their ignorance that they cannot be trusted with greater responsibilities. With his clairvoyant knowledge the Master will discover the exact spiritual status of the student and instruct him accordingly, assisting him to strengthen the weak points and round out the invisible side of his nature. The work for each disciple is absolutely individual and hence differs from that of all other disciples. In all this world there are no two people constituted exactly alike. The physical body merely bears witness and molds itself into the pattern of the spiritual organism. Therefore this   individuality merely proves the absolute individuality of each spiritual organism.

No one but a moral murderer or an unmitigated ignoramus would attempt to prescribe one medicine for all cases. Anyone who writes a book for general circulation telling an individual how to develop his spiritual sight must remember that thousands of people, no two of them alike, will read it, and many will destroy themselves in seeking to follow instructions which were not intended for them. Such an individual would thus prove conclusively that he was mentally unfitted to receive the instructions in the beginning or he would certainly have retained sufficient intelligence to use them more wisely.

The true Masters never appear in public teaching large classes or groups concerning occult exercises, but come privately to their disciples and instruct each one individually. The ability to inform the disciple concerning the steps to be taken before his actual initiation is the result of the high degree of development reached by the Adept. None who is not an Adept is able to prescribe for the spiritual needs of students without assuming heavy Karmic responsibilities. The disciple will probably be visited at night by his Teacher, who will come in a superphysical body. The student will feel certain that he is fully awake, and in a spiritual sense of the word he is, but he will recognize the Master only through superphysical vision. If he has not developed his spiritual nature by right living, right thinking and right feeling during his probation as a student, he will be unable to recognize the Master when he comes.

The work of the disciple is to learn unquestioning obedience. As the child obeys its father, so must he obey his Master once that Master has proven his authority and his virtue. To disobey the Master in even the slightest particular is to be separated from him possibly for the rest of his life. The student must obey unquestioningly the instruction which he receives. To deviate from it in even the slightest detail may prove fatal to himself. His work as a disciple is to prepare his embryonic superphysical bodies so that when he is an Initiate he may use them as vehicles of consciousness.

The third degree is that of Initiate. In this grade are the accepted and proven disciples who, while out of the physical body, under the direction of their Teachers, have actually and consciously taken one or more initiations in the invisible Temple of a true Mystery School. There are no spiritual initiations given in the physical world. All the true initiations must take place in the invisible worlds, for that is the only place where there can be found those authorized and fitted to give them. The forms and rituals used here are all exoteric and only symbolic of the true spiritual rituals used in the Mystery Temples. Today even the rituals mean very little, for in the majority of cases the student has not only lost the meaning of the symbolic services, but he has also forgotten that they had an inner significance. As Eliphas Levi, the great transcendentalist, has well said, the tests and obligations of the Mystery Schools are no longer given because none are sufficiently illumined to understand their inner significance. Therefore, none are willing to go through their hardships only to find that their ignorance will remain unenlightened. This is the great fault which mystics find with the religions in the world today. In the majority of cases they are pageantries of empty words.

On the threshold between the visible and the invisible worlds stands the Dweller, which Lord Bulwer-Lytton has so well described in his great Rosicrucian novel, *Zanoni*. This sphinx-like creature, which each must pass on his way to the Temple of Light, represents the lower nature of the candidate himself. While the consciousness is within the bodies, it cannot see this demon, but when outside it gets a detached view of itself, the lower animal nature made visible through a composite astral body is seen and recognized for the first time. This spectre the candidate must pass as he steps across from one world to the other. In order to accomplish this feat successfully, he must gain complete control over the forces in his own nature which since his first differentiation from the animal consciousness have been building the lower side of his nature. If mentally and spiritually he has mastered those elements he is strong enough to pass unmoved and unafraid before this phantom of his own perversions and enter with strength and courage into the invisible worlds.

When he is able to do this, the candidate shows that he has taken the first step toward self-mastery. Having accomplished this and learned to control his own complex organisms, he is now ready to be given power over greater things.

There are many grades of initiates, and no matter how far a seeker may pass on the pathway of understanding there is always something more for him to accomplish. We may compare it to a man walking toward the horizon. As rapidly as he approaches it, it recedes from him. No one but the Absolute itself is all-wise, all-powerful, all-knowing, or all-complete. Wisdom and ignorance are comparative terms, not only in the material world but in the spiritual world as well. The mere fact that he has been accepted by one of the Ancient Schools does not mean that the student has become all-wise. It merely gives him a little more exalted view. He merely sees life with slightly broadened vision, but he is still subject to the laws of Nature. He is still subject to faults and failings, he is still capable of failure.

With his initiations the disciple gains certain occult powers that ever increase as he advances along the pathway of adeptship. As the schools in the material world are divided into many grades, so the spiritual school in the Mystery Temple is divided into many stages and degrees. The disciple gradually passes from one initiation to another as he becomes more efficient in the labors which the invisible world expects him to accomplish. As he passes ever higher he gradually increases in power, wisdom, and understanding. Not, however, until the initiate reaches a very high degree does he become independent of the bonds that curb the ordinary human being. We may say he does not become superior to law until he becomes part of the law itself, and then he is above breaking it. Even after many initiations all the laws of human limitation hold good. Initiates are subject to birth, growth, and old age. Sickness and sorrow still confront them at every turn. They must return to this life again like other normal beings until their development carries them to a state of consciousness much higher than that which the average individual can hope to reach in one lifetime.

There are no initiates who are not clairvoyant, at least to a certain degree, for they cannot receive their spiritual ordination until they are capable of functioning consciously out of the physical body. Neither are there any true initiates who do not know their true position. Many people come and say, "I had a strange experience in my sleep. Was it an initiation?" The answer in nearly every case is negative. The initiate is in doubt neither as to what he has accomplished nor what he has been through. The average student can ask himself, "What am I here and now? Am I worthy to be picked for greater responsibility? If I were a Master, with all the world to choose from, would I choose myself for great and responsible works? If I would not, with my narrowed sight, would the Master be deceived by the slender virtues I possess and choose me when there are others much more fit?"

There are no Adepts or Masters in this world or upon the invisible planes who have not passed through all the sorrows and uncertainties of human experience. They have reached their present position because they have mastered those uncertainties and have risen above the circumstances which chain most people to the selfish side of life. All of the Great Ones have passed sequentially and gradually from ignorance to wisdom. None was made overnight. Each was tempted and each was strong through the moments of temptation. All were persecuted. Many died for their ideals, preferring wisdom above all treasure and truth above all power. Each initiate who now sits in session with the Elder Brothers has earned his position by consecration, intelligence, and sincerity. These are the magic keys which open the gates of the Mystery Schools.

Again and again the question is asked, "How can we know an initiate if we come in contact with one?" We can only answer, "By their works shall ye know them." After analyzing the lives and habits of those initiates whom we are able to recognize with our limited vision, we find that they all adhered to a general series of rules. Conditions are altered by the needs of the moment, but among the ancient manifestos we find hints as to the conduct of adepts and mystics.

For many hundreds of years the true Adepts and Initiates shrouded themselves in an impenetrable veil of mystery. This procedure served many ends. First, it protected the Initiates from the endless inconveniences to which they would be subjected by the curious and the credulous. It also permitted them to live quietly and silently, to study and pray, unknown and unsuspected even by their next door neighbor. Then, again, it multiplied the power which they had over a world which could not oppose them because it could not discover them. And, lastly, it enabled these schools and their disciples to escape the persecutions of religious bigotry and intolerance that have always been felt when man sought to discover God without benefit of clergy.

The Egyptian Sphinx is supposed to have pointed out the initiate's code of conduct by the symbolic interpretation of the four creatures composing it. The body of the bull with its great strength was interpreted to mean the process of labor, "to do." The legs and tail of the lion speak of courage and are interpreted as meaning "to dare." The wings of the eagle bespeak of loftier things, so they are interpreted as "to aspire." The human head, with its sealed lips, means "to be silent." Of all these rules, the last is the most important.

One of the ancient occult axioms was, "If ye know it, be silent." Today in both the orthodox and occult worlds of religious thought there is entirely too much talking. There are too many claiming powers and virtues which they do not possess. Places of worship have become institutions of debate, while cliques and clans are breaking off in all directions because idealism has been wrecked on the rocks of petty personality. There is a surfeit of initiates, but little wisdom. There is a multitude of pedagogues and demigods, but all together cannot keep peace in their own ranks, let alone convert the Gentiles. Nearly all this comes from too much talking, and making light of serious matters. The names of the Masters have been dragged in the mud. The Mystery Schools have merely become part of the paraphernalia with which to juggle commercial psychology, and the spirit of reverence and love which the ancient world felt for its initiates has been lost in our day because of the host of false initiates and fraudulent psychologists.

A true occultist, be he student, disciple, or initiate, never discloses his position to any except those equally interested and equally sincere along similar lines. He should do his work incognito, veiling the truths he has learned in the simple language of the street, telling men what they should do, not what he himself is; urging, suggesting, but never forcing either his opinions or his philosophies upon others; neither is he puffed up by applause nor disheartened by criticism. He should labor quietly in the field where he finds himself. He should always be inconspicuous, silent, and unobtrusive. He should labor diligently, allowing his work and not his tongue to speak for him.

An initiate or disciple should never state his position publicly, nor should he discuss his spiritual aspirations. If he has been privileged to view spiritual phenomena in his own life, if he has been taken out of his body or is developing clairvoyant powers, those are the most sacred things in his life. They should never be spoken of in public, for they are sacred to him and his Master. To discuss personal powers is the worst breach of etiquette conceivable in the occult world.

Looking back over the lives of Initiates we note several things concerning which they were most exacting. We are sorry to find that students of today are rather lax in these things. Therefore, we suggest for your consideration the following:

(a) All true occultists abide by the laws of the nations and the community in which they dwell. While in many cases they recognize these laws as imperfect, they abide by them lest by their moral example they should teach the less intelligent to break the restraining bonds of law and order. It is said that laws are made for those who break them. We may add that laws were not made for Initiates, but there is a very small minority of people intelligent enough to live together honestly without the assistance of law. No matter how bad these laws are, they are far superior to the lawlessness which would exist when the mental hazard of punishment is removed from the untrained and unregenerated man.

From time to time occultists are dragged into court because they have failed to set a good example to their fellow creatures. There is no doubt that the element of persecution which existed in the Middle Ages is still to be found in places and that many are unjustly persecuted. But still there are entirely too many who, feeling that their spirituality is superior to that of their fellow creatures, deliberately ignore the law. Especially is this true with the wildly fantastic soul-mate and free-love institutions. These things are not sanctioned under any conditions by the Ancient Wisdom, for the Mystery Schools themselves instituted the legal bond of matrimony. Anything which suggests the breaking of existing laws without first preparing a better law for the mass of the uninformed is outside the pale of the Ancient Wisdom.

(b) True occultists break no laws, regardless of how unjust they may be. If they see injustice, they labor to introduce more just legislation. A notable example of this is found in the life of Abraham Lincoln. Many times slaves came to him before the Civil War begging him to assist them to escape from their lives of servitude. This Lincoln refused to do, because it was against the law, but he told them that while he would never break the existing statutes he would consecrate his life to making a better law. It is in this spirit that all occultists must work with injustice, for in this way truth is established without the rioting and Bolshevism of lawlessness.

(c) All occultists and initiates should assume the dress and customs of the nation or people among whom they dwell, lest any departure from that custom shall cause them to be unduly conspicuous. This was one of the strictest rules of the Ancient Wisdom teachers, and is found among the old manifestoes of the Rosicrucian brotherhood.

(d) The true Adept and Initiate shall reveal his identity to no man, unless that one is worthy to receive it. The secret work which they have been permitted to have is a two-edged sword. When they had prepared themselves to receive it, it was good for them, but by promiscuously giving it to others they could do great harm. Therefore, they reveal to no man the secret instructions they have received nor the source from whence it came, being satisfied to disseminate it quietly and inconspicuously. When questioned concerning these things, they state their position and then remain silent. This privilege to remain silent they defend with their lives.

(e) The true Initiate and disciple shall never be boisterous or declamatory in his statements, nor radical in his viewpoints, nor encourage such conditions among those with whom he comes in contact, nor speak for his organization or his Masters. The true Initiate has no will but the will of his Masters, nor does he palm off his own judgment as having any more important origin than his own brain. He must take no radical steps unless commanded to do so by the Great Brothers who have the lives of men in their care.

(f) When dwelling in a community, Initiates shall be peace-loving, simple, kindly, charitable, and not critical of those about them, making themselves invaluable through their intelligence and their integrity. They shall watch their conduct day and night that it may in no way reflect against the exalted organization of which they bear witness. They shall be humble in all things, willing and glad to do the most menial labor if it will add to the welfare and progress of their fellow creatures. It shall be said of such a one, as of the Master Jesus that he went about doing good.

(g) Under no conditions shall they use any of the spiritual powers which they may possess for their own aggrandizement or protection, unless such is for the unselfish good of others. It is against all the laws of occultism to apply any knowledge which is of a supernatural nature for the salvation, preservation, or improvement of self. As stated of the Master Jesus, others He could help but Himself He could not save. For this reason modern psychology and mental magic of various kinds are contrary to the orders of the Ancient Wisdom; for by modern psychologists the student is taught these spiritual gifts that he may use for his own aggrandizement.

(h) Under no condition is the teacher warranted in exacting pay for the spiritual instructions which he gives, for no money was paid to receive them nor is any coin of the realm a payment for them. The student assumes his share of responsibility, and ingratitude is one of the major sins of occultism. When a student who is in a position to assist retards, through his miserliness, the work of the Master, such a one assumes all the Karmic debts incurred as the result of his failure to cooperate. No student should study occultism with the object of using it as a commercial enterprise. Such will never see either the Masters or the Temple.

The foregoing may throw some light on the reason why it is so difficult to determine the position of the ancient initiates. Their reticence and humble spirit have seldom found a place on the pages of history, and yet they are the real molders of the destinies of nations. They are the invisible powers behind the thrones of earth, and men are but marionettes, dancing while the invisible ones pull the strings. We see the dancer, but the master mind that does the work remains concealed by the cloak of silence.

A follower of the Master or of any of the seven Great Schools which they have established in order to disseminate the Ancient Wisdom, is not privileged to call himself a member of any occult order or school until he has passed one or more actual initiations in the spiritual Temple of the order to which he has been drawn by his planetary lights. The reading of literature, the payment of fees, or the signing of pledges does not make the student an occultist or a member of any of the true spiritual orders. Only by the first initiation in the spiritual Temple is he made a true member. He may join this society, that organization or the other brotherhood, and so state, but he is thus affiliating himself with only an exoteric order. His true membership comes with his entrance into the Temple which contains the spiritual hierarchy that animates and vivifies the outer material institution.

Time and time again we find students, disciples, and even initiates of the lower orders who, through a certain remnant of egotism still remaining in their natures, have brought disgrace upon the thing which they truly love. This usually results from some ignominious failure which they make and which, because they have incessantly emphasized their spiritual position, is laid at the door of the school which they claim to represent. With a slight revision of Scriptural phraseology, today many people say, "What good thing can come out of occultism?" This attitude is the result of the great spiritual schools being humiliated again and again by the abject failure of some of their disciples. This condition is largely the result of egotism, for the disciple was unable to stand a little dignity without making sure that everyone knew about it. Egotism is one of the most serious of human failings that the occultist has to overcome, for it makes him insensible to his own worthiness, of which no true disciple should ever lose sight.

In this day of religious thought, most people desire to belong to something. Like barnacles they attach themselves to the ship of human progress and finally, when a sufficient number of these crustaceans have attached themselves with their hard-shelled opinions, the ship either sinks under the weight, or, like some of our occult organizations, must go into drydock and have its incrustations removed. When you claim membership in anything, ask yourself whether that institution is as proud of having you as a member as you are of claiming membership in it. Most people join spiritual movements to gain something for themselves. They become parasites, living off a Tree of Wisdom which another man has planted and cultivated. True people affiliate themselves with the Mystery Schools not to better themselves but to serve that institution faithfully and well. Until they feel that they are a credit to it in every sense of the word, they do not wish to   have their name linked with that of which they are not a worthy representative.

Instead of claiming membership in this, that or the other and thus casting reflection upon the integrity of the Masters, let us take another of the ancient rules for our standard and in this way uphold the dignity of the superior thing. Let us suppose that you have just joined the ancient religious order which was called Gnosticism.

We have said that there were three divisions—students, disciples and initiates. Let us see how we should state our position if we were to attain any one of those three degrees in the ancient religion of the Gnostics.

If a student, we would say, "I am a student of the Gnostic philosophy." If a disciple, we would say, "I am a disciple of the Gnostic path of wisdom." If an initiate admitted into the spiritual Temple of the Gnosis, we would say, "I am a Gnostic." In this last simple statement we have distinctly affiliated ourselves with the spiritual hierarchy manipulating the Gnostic order. We would never say that we were anything unless actually initiated into the esoteric organization, which, concealed behind the exoteric order, is in every case the true institution of which the exoteric structure is but the symbol.

Every member of an occult organization should make his position unmistakably clear. He owes this not only to the order but also to himself, for daily misunderstandings arise because students are not honest enough to admit themselves to be merely seekers and not adepts in disguise. The Ancient Wisdom demands honesty and would have in its ranks none without sufficient love for the order to defend it from every calumny and bear upon their own shoulders, if necessary, its honor and integrity.

Why should people try to be virtuous when they see others pass on to wisdom with all their sins? The high standards of the Wisdom Schools are discredited by persons who, while full of faults, claim to be initiated members in good standing of an organization which stands for all that is high and noble. In the name of the Great Work, it is wise to admit that all we have of virtue we owe to the Masters and their instructions, while for our vices we are indebted to our own lower natures. This attitude will serve the Great Work far better than you will ever know.

Lightning Source UK Ltd.
Milton Keynes UK
UKHW041821150719
346204UK00003B/134/P